COMBATTING WASTEFULNESS & COVID-19 ETC.

Seton During

Published by New Generation Publishing in 2022

Copyright © Seton During 2022

First Edition

The author asserts the moral right under the Copyright, Designs and Patents Act 1988 to be identified as the author of this work.

All Rights reserved. No part of this publication may be reproduced, stored in a retrieval system or transmitted, in any form or by any means without the prior consent of the author, nor be otherwise circulated in any form of binding or cover other than that which it is published and without a similar condition being imposed on the subsequent purchaser.

ISBN
   Paperback 978-1-80369-238-8
   Hardback   978-1-80369-239-5
   Ebook   978-1-80369-252-4

www.newgeneration-publishing.com

Seton During's Book titled "**ANTI-WASTEFULNESSES & ANTI-COVID**" with unpleasant contemporaneous realities to be combatted by victims!

Dedication

This book is dedicated to **ethical taxpayers worldwide;** with costs-conscious progressives in the domestic, public, private, voluntary, and foreign sectors; the ignored should also benefit.

It disproportionally concentrates on errors of omission and commission to highlight, create, and confirm awareness and motivate corrections with strategies, policies, and practices for stopping their recurrences.

Foreword

This is an attempt to highlight some aspects and happenstances of operational management which can be improved for the benefit of most and to inspire optimising reappraisals for attention.

The author is an 84-year-old chartered marine engineer, chartered plant engineer, and an assessor of mature candidates for chartered status of the Institution of Plant Engineers in the UK, a voluntary sector activist, ex-London Borough of Enfield councillor, ex-justice of the peace, ex- UK political constituencies' treasurer - Edmonton Labour Party & North London UKIP (United Kingdom Independence Party) – five altogether – one-at-a-time.

Currently Deputy Chairman of United Kingdom CANCER BLACK CARE. Prostate Cancer survivor via brachytherapy (-not recommended), and Alzheimer's disease survivor.

Chapter 1

Some notions for you to consider.

Respect governments because we have not yet evolved credible and better alternatives but never trust them one hundred per cent, the same with the police because they have an unknown percentage of undesirables among them who they have not yet been able to identify and extricate!

Protect yourself from undesirable afflictions by seriously considering taking credible prophylactics, and auto-immune boosters – available on the internet but not available on our UK NHS; discuss this with your GP.

Your natural immune system you acquired and have developed since birth peaks at about your 19th birthday and its effectiveness begins to wane soon after. This is an open secret your GPs, medical consultants and pharmacists had not been telling you much because such beneficial knowledge and practices will threaten their employment prospects with reductions in pharmaceutical drugs sales and profits.

Consider discussing the following boosters etc. with your GP, although they might not be available on our UK NHS, they are online – the blessed Internet:-

a) Metatone at £7.00p per 500ml bottle – buy 2 bottles get a third one free.
b) IP6 + Inositol.
c) Maitake D-Fraction.
d) MGN3 Extra – banned in The USA, because it makes people too well thereby undermining BIG PHARMAS' sales and profits – they are unethically misperceiving such as unwelcome competition!
e) Eat and drink West African bitter leaves soups about twice a week to complement your natural ammunition, research other edible vegetation.
f) Stop smoking cigarettes, stop using cannabis sativa, stop using cocaine, and all other injurious substances COMPLETELY.
g) Reduce alcoholic drinks substantially – beverages and spirits, excluding a half-teaspoonful of exquisite communion wines once a week in churches, enlightened and progressive temples,

mosques and synagogues about whom unconfirmed rumours abound about their secretly imbibing.

I seek to reduce your utilities bills as I list below:-

1. Carry out your water leakages test to ensure there are no invisible leaks. With no one using water from domestic etc. outlets for one night between midnight and 5 am; read your water meter at these times, if the reading at 5 am is higher than at preceding midnight, you have an invisible leak – often from vaporising hairline and other cracks, corroded underground pipes, etc. Get quotations from registered plumbers to investigate; recommendations preferred and obtain written quotes firstly.
2. Access the spaces between highest ceilings and roof, if you can see the sky anywhere, you have a leaking roof and heat loss source. While you are still there, inspect the roof void/loft insulation and repair as required; or, if none exists, install it – your spending here is actually an investment yielding savings continually as dividends.

3. Instead of turning up your thermostat, put on a woollen jumper.
4. Leave the car at home for short journeys.
5. Install hot water and photovoltaic solar panels.
6. Choose energy-saving light bulbs.
7. Take showers – with low flow shower heads – DO NOT take baths.
8. Install a water butt for watering your garden.
9. Exploiting the virtues of the Internet, by considering tips available online from the Energy Saving Trust, the Citizens Advice Bureau, Smart Energy GB, etc., such opportunities are limitless.
10. Triple glaze doors and windows.
11. Install draughtproofing, including locks keyholes in external front, back and side doors leading into your garage.
12. Save on heating bills by exploiting opportunities in the two rooms you occupy mostly – your bedroom, and, your day room. Turn the thermostats in your bedroom and dayroom down to 18 and 21 degrees Centigrade respectively.
13. While inside your house, place the back of your palm about an eighth of an inch

from each external door – front leading out, back leading into your garden, and side leading into your garage; if you feel any draughts, change to draught-proof lock/s.

14. Coax all our MPs, the prime minister, the cabinet secretary, and particularly finance ministers to ascertain what happens to monies **retained** by banks because of their discovering anomalies about the cheque signatories, and various other reasons such as payees-banks returning payments, etc.? How and who do they account to statutory bodies outside banking for such monies, e.g. deceased who die intestate without next of kin - this may reduce taxes!

15. Relevant but perhaps extraneous is a current PPI (Public Private Initiative) untapped opportunity for reducing our NHS treatment of dementia patients by investing in joint research into using Infrared Light PBM-T (transcranial photobiomodulation) therapy which stimulates the mitochondria for treatment of dementia patients; consider contacting the pilot study researchers Dr. Paul Chazot, Durham University

UK, and Dr. Gordon Dougal of Maculume Ltd., about their specially designed helmet for this purpose.

16. Look for loose roof tiles
17. Clear gutters.
18. Ensure gates and fences are secure.
19. Trim back overhanging branches.
20. Secure outdoor furniture
21. Get a Registered Gas Safe technician to service your heating and hot water boiler – costs about £65.
22. Bleed radiators – starting from the lowest then moving upwards.
23. Ensure all your pipework is insulated
24. Draught-proof your home.
25. Re-appraise all your contractual documents - home, and car etc. insurances; insert renewal dates in next year's diary. It may be better to put all such payments on a rolling direct debit or standing order, including subscriptions.
26. Get your chimneys swept.
27. Install cavity wall insulation.
28. Choose photovoltaic solar panels to complement your heating and hot water needs.
29. Opt for triple glazed windows and doors.

30. Turn appliances off – do not leave them on stand-by.
31. Remind your local authority chief executive and councillors about CHP (combined heat & power) installations maintenance and allied management.
32. -----------ditto------------power factor correctors; confess your interest in reducing your council tax here and about item 31 above.
33. Visit your library and the Internet for more tips…
34. Leave frozen food out overnight to defrost – for as and when required.
35. Become an activist about promoting reductions of heating and electricity bills by installing CHP (Combined Heat & Power); and Electrical Power Factor Reductions Units as economically applicable. Continue reminding property owners about their maintenance management and relevant statutory and mandatory compliances - often disgracefully neglected – with HM Treasury and Auditors evading and avoiding commensurate actions!

The current and on-going so-called COVID-19 virus – with its variants - formerly named 2019-

nCoV from an alleged inception origin in Fort Detrick, Frederick, Maryland, USA: note that this ethically contradicts the preferred propaganda that it originated from Wuhan City within Hubei Province in China by occidental media barons with deleterious privately financed propaganda by the super-rich. They promoted their misperception of the majority poor from menace to threat to be profitably decimated – by developing and spreading this and other man-made viruses. COVID-19 is curable because developed ANTIDOTES exist which had also been simultaneously developed for the benefits of preferred victims and sharing secretly amongst rich individuals in the ratio 7:2:1:: **ONE:TWO:THREE countries** excluding government officers in **these countries**.

Remember that HIV, Aids, Ebola and now Covid-19 with mutating variants (originally named 2019-nCoV) have all originated from one country out of the 196 recognised by the United Nations and were each designed for selective human decimation, or depopulation, or egalitarian racism to wipe-out those misperceived as undesirables by the diseases' originators, whose GREEDY – very

HITLERITE – eugenics drove their selective depopulation agenda.

COVID-19 mutates into new variants for which efficacious vaccines are yet to be satisfactorily developed.

Constituents of exported vaccines can be varied according to the intended or preferred impact on the importing nation – the evil wrongdoers!

December 2021 - note that with low vaccination rates, Africa's covid deaths remain far below those of Europe and the United States; while Africa's population is 16% of the world's total, covid deaths in Africa make up 2.9% - puzzling – even allowing for lower standards of statistics and records-keeping!

Has anyone tabulated the qualities of natural immunity imbued amongst sub-Saharan Africans – birthed with higher percentages of Vitamins D, C, and zinc – for example.

The greedy dominance of capitalist profiteering imperatives along with the inordinate levels of political misinformation and misdirection adversely affect developments of coherent, effective public health strategies with allied social policies.

Steve Hirsch intimates that the statistician Mathew Crawford has graphically demonstrated that these evildoers are killing 150000 persons to save no one.

Please consider reading Jessica Rose's, Steffanie Seneff's, and Bart Classen's three individual papers about linking some of these mRNA COVID vaccines with incurable often fatal Prion diseases – these revelations are being suppressed.

An anonymous Indian posted an apology after revealing that Fort Detrick via Nallin Farm Gate within Frederick in Maryland USA played an evil part in the development and outbreak of COVID-19; his immediate supervisor was Professor Frank Plummer (- of GS-5734 fame) who knew the most about these things had been quietly assassinated while flying from Kenya to China to meet with his Chinese counterpart – one of his best friends included Professor Ralph S. Baric!

Pure and applied scientists with evil governments continue loudly quiet about all such assassinations!

It continues to appear that deaths from the vaccines which primarily attack their victims' natural immune systems by triggering over-defensive responses are higher than deaths from the virus itself.

Has anyone looked properly into the rise in the number of still births in Canada - being suppressed – you guessed it?

All current vaccines are "RUSHED" because none has so far satisfactorily completed the six stages – Zero to 5 - essential for credible verifications; they are all mostly at Stage 3, so we the currently vaccinated are their guinea pigs.

Their efficacies are time-limited, this explains why the fraudsters persistently dictate that you take extra jabs – second, third, etc. boosters – excellent for their sales and profits. Bad for our National Deficit!

Have you noticed how BIG PHARMAS' stocks, shares and dividends still continue to rise – they are raking in fortunes from us taxpayers because all our politicians are complacently ignorant? They lazily accept what the private sector drug manufacturers tell them.

Their gambling has been imposed on the public and private sector scientists who have neither got nor been given the essential full details of all the constituents of the formulae with other ingredients and stages with CPA (critical path analyses) and allied Gantt/bar charts employed in progressing the development of this VIRUS, so they continue working blindly and in the dark.

Statistically, we may be killing 150,000 people to save zero lives – please consider reading Mathew Crawford's data from UK Analysis: thanks to Steve Kirsch.

May 13^{th,} 2021, the Seychelles – an archipelago of 115 islands populated by about 98,000 – was perhaps the most vaccinated at 70% and rising; later, about a third of new COVID-19 victims who had been fully vaccinated became virus victims!

September 11th, 2021, none of these vaccines stopped severe COVID or deaths!

November 20th, 2021, the USA's Dr Anthony Fauci (finally admitted vaccines do not protect against serious COVID or death)!

Recently, the CDC (Centre for Diseases Control in Atlanta, Georgia) approved a fourth shot for the vulnerable – implying that the previous three might be fakes or had waned too fast or too quickly.

Nobody knows what the adverse long-term effects on human brain cells, the nervous systems, and reproductive organs from imbibing these rushed vaccines might be.

We have not been told that some of these new COVID at-home test kits might be dangerous because some might contain dangerous Sodium Azide (chemical formula NaN_3), a potentially deadly chemical not to be confused with Sodium Nitride (chemical formula Na_3N).

Russians, Africans, Europeans, Muslims, Indians, Chinese, South Americans,

Australians and Canadians were not involved in the 2019-nCoV January 2019 to July/August 2019 developmental stages.

Fort Detrick was shut down during July/August 2019 after threats by whistleblowers!

Do not trust any politician because their pre-eminent twinned priority is winning their next elections and lining their pockets, not optimising the quality of your health and well-being. They are clueless about epidemiology!

Similarly, pharmaceutical multinationals whose topmost priority is PROFIT even at the expense of your health and life.

You should not be surprised that some of these mRNA vaccines being touted contain latent prion disease/s' ingredients – these are transmissible spongiform encephalopathies (TSEs), a family of rare progressive neurodegenerative disorders distinguished by long incubation periods – which lead to incurable Alzheimer's disease followed more often than not by dementia then death!

The scientists who secretly developed EBOLA within a country outside of Africa before transportation to Africa included Jonathan S. Towner, Stuart T. Nichol, James A. Comer, Thomas G. Kalazek, and Pierre E. Rollin – the US Patent No. is CA2741523A1.

The names of the 53 pure and applied scientists including auxiliaries and ancillaries - who allegedly developed COVID-19 (- originally named 2019-nCoV) at Fort Detrick within Frederick in Maryland USA will be forwarded as soon as I receive them from ethical dissidents and mistreated auxiliary and ancillary staff who are misnamed as traitors by some Hitlerite Americans.

America has 17 separate intelligence agencies; tasked with determining the origins of COVID by current President Biden resulted in all of them collectively asserting "We don't know" – tactfully civil-servicy.

In 2017, Trump recruited Robert Kadlec – a leading American biowarfare advocate; after which in 2018 a mysterious viral epidemic hit China's poultry industry; in 2019, another viral epidemic hit China's pork industry, now, work out the sources/origins of these man-made viral attacks!

In Germany, the states with the highest vaccination rates have the most deaths; what does this tell you?

In the absence of any tested and proven cure here in the UK and with my merchant navy background, I have opted for and prefer practical prevention or prophylactics, so I practise using POVIDONE IODINE - **$C_6H_9I_2NO$** - Spray because Iodine and its derivatives kill COVID-19; why it had not been tested for anti-COVID-19 efficacy within buildings' HVAC (heating, ventilation and air-conditioning) Systems sprayed into air-supply ducts after HEPA (high efficiency particulate air) filters within these ducts here in the UK baffles me – it craves and merits investigative Pilot Projects at least!

Fact 1. COVID-19 had been privately funded by private billionaires so the American taxpayers with their clever Joint Chiefs of Staff are absolved of responsibilities for its creation and no public audit, and/or accountability can be satisfactorily carried out.

The Joint Chiefs of Staff tactful escapology was – Yes, Mr President, but as this had not been budgeted for, we need to go to Congress and plead for the extra/new funding and warning that we may be back for more due to the emergences of the inevitable unforeseen variations as there are no knowings of what this adventure might entail!

The President negated this going to Congress for funding because it would undermine essential secrecy, this is why 2019-nCoV (COVID-19's original name) was "privately funded". This is the world we live in! **All these from an alleged and uncertain Jewish-American President – bettering Hitler.** His election educates the rest of the world about the unreliability of America.

Fact 2. Occidental media barons breathing down the necks of editors practically block pertinent questions such as:-

a) Why were these MAN-MADE viruses developed, and who developed them? Prime suspects appear to lead to rich Americans who escalated their misperception of the poor from menace to threat; they continue to be highly and greedily intolerant of an internal NHSs (National Health Services) for all Americans.

b) Who are targeted? Primarily, non-whites – starting with the Chinese, followed by sub-Saharan Africans, then the aged – to reduce national public sector pensioners' bills and invoices; followed by all with weak or compromised natural immune systems? **It is now boomeranging uncontrollably and internationally with mutating variants!**

c) Had The CIA (Central Intelligence Agency) and/or The NIH (National Institutes of Health in Bethesda, Maryland) and/or The CDC (Centre for Diseases Control) in Georgia, USA for years been secretly funding China's own WMD (Weapons of Mass Destruction) plus GW (Germ Warfare) facility in Wuhan within Hubei Province in China without the official knowledge of both The US and Chinese Governments – allegedly since 2014 - *mirabile dictu*? **Yes, they had; ostensibly to carry out tests in Wuhan which were statutorily and/or mandatorily**

disallowed in The USA – illegal in the USA. You now know about another vehicle of how 2019-nCoV got into China.

d) The head of the CIA (Central Intelligence Agency) is appointed by The President, but this internationally ubiquitous CIA organisation is neither responsible to nor accountable to anyone anywhere?

e) have the Chinese now completed identifications of unauthorised Chinese liaisons with CIA operatives; and dealt with them quietly "Chinese Style" – they have now ceased answering their home or workplace telephones; - still in progress.

f) had the unit dedicated exclusively to this COVID-19 Project at Fort Detrick WMD (Weapons of Mass Destruction) + GW (Germ Warfare) facility within Frederick in Maryland, USA been quietly and secretly shut down in July/August 2019 because native ethical dissidents – BLESS THEM - had confirmed illicit hazardous wastes disposal contraventions and they had threatened to blow whistles; in ensuing panic, all military scientists were hurriedly returned/re-dispersed to their original Military Units they had been seconded from with HUGE UNTRACEABLE $CASH KEEP-QUIET $BONUSES?

In order to protect secrecy, they had not contracted the disposals of the ensuing hazardous wastes and allied effluents during their operations to any of the statutorily authorised specialist contractors!

Note that private and voluntary and foreign sector scientists – pharmacologists, epidemiologists, etc. had been excluded from THIS PROJECT. It was they who discovered that private legally licensed hazardous wastes disposal contractors in the US had not been statutorily contracted; all the wastes and effluents were being dumped into internal sinks to protect and sustain secrecy, ending up in sewerage systems without warning the applicable sewerage systems organisations and staff.

Some Frederick residents and their medical doctors had also been complaining about strange flus with inexplicable upper respiratory tract

afflictions – these complainants were cash-silenced with subtle threats!
g) the original name 2019-nCoV was changed to COVID-19 because it did not roll off the tongue easily and was not computer-friendly.

EDMONTON
ROLL OF HONOUR

Edmonton Urban District Council erected this Memorial Screen in Edmonton Town Hall in 1913 to commemorate acts of bravery by local people.

The restoration in 1994 was due to the support and donations of:

Focus on Edmonton
Mr F Coates
The Letch Family
Councillor J Connew
Councillor S During
Councillor G Eustance
Councillor G Loake
Councillor L Mason
Councillor A Nicholas
Councillor S Walker
The Enfield Rotary Club

CAMERAS ARE NOT PERMITTED

1993

PERSONAL CARD

HER MAJESTY'S GARDEN PARTY
AT
BUCKINGHAM PALACE

TUESDAY, 13th JULY, 1993

Mr. Seton Dusing

Please see Notes on the reverse

*The Lord Chamberlain is
commanded by Her Majesty to invite*

Mr. and Mrs. Seton Dusing

to a Garden Party at Buckingham Palace
on Tuesday, 13th July, 1993, from 4 to 6 p.m.

Morning Dress, Uniform or Lounge Suit

EııR

The Lord Chamberlain is
commanded by Her Majesty to invite

Mr. Seton and Councillor Mrs. Baring

to a Garden Party
at Buckingham Palace
on Thursday, 21st July 2005 from 4 to 6 pm

CAMERAS ARE NOT PERMITTED
MOBILE TELEPHONES ARE TO BE SWITCHED OFF

PERSONAL CARD

HER MAJESTY'S GARDEN PARTY
AT BUCKINGHAM PALACE
THURSDAY, 21ST JULY, 2005

Mr. Seton Baring

Please bring two forms of identity with you, one of which must be photographic (driving licence, passport) and the other showing your name and address (utility bill, bank statement), should the Police request to see it.

Please see Dress and Notes on the reverse

CAMERAS ARE NOT PERMITTED
MOBILE TELEPHONES ARE TO BE SWITCHED OFF

PERSONAL CARD

HER MAJESTY'S GARDEN PARTY
AT BUCKINGHAM PALACE
THURSDAY, 21ST JULY, 2005

Councillor Mrs. Baring

Please bring two forms of identity with you, one of which must be photographic (driving licence, passport) and the other showing your name and address (utility bill, bank statement), should the Police request to see it.

Please see Dress and Notes on the reverse

Chapter 2

How did it get into China then spread worldwide?

The military scientists did not realise that there were more Chinese Dollar Millionaires now flying about internationally than American ones – the sting in the tail is an extremely high percentage of these Chinese millionaires now carry American Passports because they had been born in The USA or naturalised, so they are able to travel in and out of The USA – and some of them being asymptomatic!

This problem of how to poison the Chinese was solved by exploiting the then impending October 2019 South East Asia Military Athletics Games/Competition – a sort of mini-Olympics – in which about 54 nations including the USA took part – the USA had interests in establishing a military presence in the South China Sea and of building the progressive encirclement of China which it saw as a military and economic threat – Chinese work ethic, unanimity, compliance characteristics, governmental control of labour costs, exploitation of equal opportunities to optimise productivity are aspects which Americans could not successfully compete with. *I saw and experienced all these and more during my invitation to China in 2010 and 2011 – being based in Huang Dong.*

An interesting and educative experience was I was taken to a meeting of Party bosses and entrepreneurs to talk about assistance with taxes whenever their companies make losses; the lead spokesperson for the Party bosses quietly and courteously explained that China was a Communist Country with Communist leadership, you insisted on practising capitalism which we acquiesced to, and supported some of you with START-UP LOANS, we welcome taxable profits from which all of us benefit. Losses are your creation and responsibility which we will neither subsidise nor encourage because these are against our national interests – difficult to find faults with such clever socio-politico-economic explanatory escapism!

365 Americans arrived in Wuhan during October 2019 in four flights ostensibly to take part in these Games carrying four batches of these COVID-19 viruses – Chinese and

British Intelligence services were successfully hoodwinked by our American allies about these 365 arrivals.

171 out of 365 practically competed; at the completion of these games and after the tallying of the points, the USA incredibly achieved a lowly 35th position out of about 54 competing countries which confirms the suspicion that their participation in these Games had been a low priority.

All the Americans flew out of Wuhan on 29th October 2019 escaping becoming victims of the viral infection although they did have THE ANTIDOTE.

This begs the question of what the 194 non-competing Americans had been up to, even after making allowances for athletes' support personnel?

The spreading of the disease by designed CPAs (Critical Path Analyses) allied to pertinent Gantt/bar charts with provisional contingency plans was initiated and implemented. But, what we simultaneously had were one-track-minded American military strategists and practitioners blundering about with their narrow, hollow, and shallow minds among foreigners and matters which exclude using military materiel. They either did not know or forgot that there were then and are now millions of Chinese Dollar millionaires - some carrying American Passports flying worldwide and would be spreading this MAN-MADE virus – a plague by my reckoning!

Considerations had not been accorded to the asymptomatic.

The genie is out of the bottle and could not be put back in.
Factually, China is still not culpable as the originator. Only one other country is and continues to be culpable.

This virus mutates and transforms to variants to such an extent that by the time you introduce any "RUSHED VACCINE", it has transformed into some different variants, rendering any such vaccine redundant. None of the current vaccines have successfully completed all six stages essential for credibility and efficacy; most have attained stage 3 which makes those vaccinated into guinea pigs; The effectiveness of these vaccines is allegedly limited to lasting under six months and none is 100% efficient or efficacious or effective indefinitely.

Who are profiting out of all these evil viruses? BIG PHARMA (Pharmaceutical Multinationals) bleeding victimised taxpayers' treasuries worldwide!

The peoples of so-called developing countries peoples – particularly those without reliable national 24/7 electricity supplies for sustaining essential refrigeration of the stored vaccines continuously - for whom it was and is intended will suffer the most! Most do not have solar-powered fridges.

A British Prime Minister – the late Edward Heath – coined a pertinent and apt phrase "the unacceptable face of capitalism"; in this case, capitalism firstly evolves the virus then sells the vaccines exclusively to those who can afford them letting those who cannot afford them perish; the privately owned pharmaceutical companies' profits and dividends continue to rise at the expense of the taxpayers who end up

paying the invoices the captured governments are being billed!

From about mid-November 2019, Chinese pathologists started reporting baffling human deaths due to strange and untreatable upper respiratory tract infections. China's political machines swung into action by issuing denials to combat **"losing face"** by publicly admitting national defeat which only made matters worse. Some of these pathologists stopped reporting for work and answering their home telephones or mobile/cell phones. Intriguing!

November 29th, 2021 - Dr Ute Bergner, a physicist who is also a member of The Thuringian State Parliament in Germany commissioned statisticians to investigate the relationship between vaccination and excess mortality in the 16 German federal states. They concluded that the states with the lowest percentage of the population vaccinated had the lowest excess mortality rate; and contrastingly, the states with the highest vaccination rate (66%) had the highest rate of excess deaths – not what you would have expected!

The Associated Press reported this November 2021 month that in spite of low vaccination rates, Africa had fewer COVID cases comparatively! Work that one out!

While writing, South Africa did the world a great favour by announcing their discovery of another new variant named OMICRON. I am grateful although racist media and governments vilified them for this contribution; they behaved similarly as China did when it alerted the world to COVID-19. We now know better!

My deductions are:-

1. These mRNA (messenger Ribonucleic Acids) vaccines are inserting weakened or inactivated germs into our bodies to trigger immune responses from our T-cells which vary wildly – according to your individual constitution - but are also erratically causing fatal prion diseases!
2. We in the UK are statistically killing people to save nobody – jettison nationalism, sentiment, and emotion then think about it ethically, rationally, and apolitically.

None of the United States of America's 17 intelligence agencies would confirm the true sole origin of COVID-19; very wise but we know why – in my village, Waterloo in Sierra Leone, West Africa, we call these GUILTY CONSCIENCES.

1. I must confess my disappointment about our UK GCHQ plus MI6 plus Cabinet Office triumvirate failure to have infiltrated Fort Derick and inform the Paymaster General with pertinent information for onward transmission to our Prime Minister about the origination of this MAN-MADE so-called COVID-19 Virus – this is why I had emailed my recommendation for their replacements to our UK Prime Minister via The Cabinet Office.
2. I have emailed my recommendations that all three professional heads – Cabinet Secretary, Heads of MI6 and GCHQ - be appropriately re-assigned/redeployed because they are under pensionable ages, and replacements should be urgently substituted.

Chapter 3

Combatting wastefulness by exploiting costs reductions opportunities, and considering our rising national debt, and national deficit!

Starting in and with the United Kingdom; and applying equal opportunities ethically, **firstly I target our Monarchy** to optimise togetherness.

On the two occasions I have been invited to meet Queen Elizabeth II and her late husband at Buckingham Palace Garden parties – see photocopies of both invitations - I had soliloquized about what I could contribute to the healthier and better maintenance of this institution – Two options topped my list: optimising energy management & energy conservation on the Crown Estates. I shall start with investigating the potentials for reducing her invoices/consumptions of fuel oils, water, gas, electricity along with whatever else I may discover without threatening statutes and desirables, e.g., the determinations of invisible water losses the estates might still be unfairly paying for – if any! Many of us are currently suffering as victims.

Excluding auxiliary and ancillary staff, I am concerned about Prince Charles' alleged intention to reduce the number of Members of our Monarchy, I suggest retaining the current number but at minus 15% of basic salaries individually before statutory deductions which would result in none of them starving, becoming homeless or destitute, and it would also improve VFM (Value for Money) of our taxes. I can see many latent beneficial potential in each and every one of them. They can then be tactfully re-deployed for promoting internal manufacturing and exports – I have stacks of nationally beneficial jobs for them. One such is coaxing all landlords to voluntarily install external ANPR (Automatic Number Plate Registration) CCTV (Closed Circuit Television) to optimise the efficacy, effectiveness, and efficiency of policing. Another is auditing Local Authorities Assets Management – combatting neglects of CHPs (combined heat & power) installations maintenance and allied management; these will need new legislation. More will of course follow.

Secondly, I now target parliament and local government!

Disappointingly, the Chancellor of The Exchequer (Chief Finance Minister) Rishi Sunak did not mention much about manufacturing and exports in his last budget speech in November 2021 – we need to resile to earnings firstly before spends. What do you think?

May I remind you about my article published in The Enfield Independent on 16th November 2016 highlighting the economic need for fewer MPs – my **article** published on page 4 of ENFIELD INDEPENDENT dated November 16th 2016 is reproduced here. I now repeat that the numbers of MPs, salaried Peers and Councillors should be reduced by a third and all the remaining ones should be on the same current basic salaries – following commensurate redrawing of boundaries by The Boundary Commission, Assembly Members would remain as they currently are.

Seton During's Article

Fewer MPs, more money saved

Draft political constituency boundary changes to reduce the total number of MPs to 600 – equalising numbers of voters per constituency as best as possible – is a step in the right direction, considering that:-

1. Our current UK National Debt is £1.6trillion and rising,
2. Our current UK National Deficit is £28.68Trillion and rising,
3. Our current UK Government sincerely pledged to reduce both.

Of course, it is not good enough for me because about six years ago, whilst my Ponders End Ward was in Enfield North Constituency, I successfully initiated these reductions during one Enfield North Conservative Party members meeting.

What I suggested were that the numbers of MPs be reduced from 650 to 443 – including the three Speakers – have you noticed how smoothly and better the country runs whilst

Parliament is in recess; and the numbers of Councillors be reduced by one-third – e.g., the London Borough of Enfield Councillors be reduced from the current bloated 63 back to 42, i.e., from 3 per ward back to VFM (Value For Money) two per ward on the same pay etc., because we cannot afford this wastefulness.

When I was a Councillor 1990 to 1994, there were 42 of us and we coped without salaries.

Within a short time of registering my suggestion, I was intimated that The Conservative Party were considering them seriously.

Later, I was intimated that the Conservatives could not progress to my figures because of their Coalition Lib-Dems' obstructionisms; but they had acquiesced to 600 MPs in The House of Commons.

You might not have noticed that successive UK Governments have failed to promote manufacturing for exports and reducing imports – I continue to notice this too.

The entire set-up needs an appraisal of VFM – value for money – based on national interests.

For contingency and forward planning, The Boundary Commission should prepare and store "management of changes plans" available for future uses – this will entail redrawing of political constituencies with wards boundaries.

Thirdly, Our Civil Service.

1. Change the designation of Permanent Secretary to General Manager.
2. Charge each of these managers to evolve - within one year - tested and proven empirical formulae for ascertaining the efficiency, effectiveness, and efficacy of every civil and public servant, Officers of the Crown along with others within ALMOs (arms' length management organisations). It may helpfully trigger a revival of the statutory 6% rate of return on capital employed for DLOs (direct labour organisations) within Local Authorities and external ALMOs.

The Unions had successfully pressured Ex-PMs Tony Blair and Gordon Brown to discard it because it had been measuring their workers' performances to our national detriment, although benefiting taxpayers.

Our private sector has profit and loss as some measure of performance – crude, but it works - but our public sector has nothing comparable!

Our HM Treasury has a bad historical habit of doling out our taxes monies without caring about how these are efficiently or inefficiently spent, e.g. Glaringly bad examples include abused subsidies for installations, operations, and maintenance of CHP (Combined Heat & Power) Installations on various estates for reducing costs of heating and electricity which most management leaderships mismanage because of their ignorance of essential maintenance management and allied terotechnology – your neither read nor heard about MPs or Councillors asking pertinent questions because of their low standards of cost consciousness, poor and low standards of relevant skills, experiences, knowledge, and education! How do I know? I had studied them at very close quarters as a London

Borough of Enfield 1990 to 1994 Councillor etc. Another is the all-sector under-exploitations of Power Factor Correctors for reducing electricity bills where economically applicable.

I had seen such due to my experiences working in various Local Authorities and The NHS.

Another is FOREIGN AID

I acquiesce with our Chancellor of The Exchequer Rishi Sunak's targeting sustenance of Foreign Aid at 0.7% of GDP in his Budget Presentation last week – in principle but not in general practice; I prefer such sustenance be rewarded by the quality of "how these monies &/or goods &/or services" are spent – considering anomalous purchasing malpractices - and publicly accounted for by recipients to both donors and receiving political elites' nationals; I would agree with 0.6% of our GDP.

Factors upon which I base FOREIGN AID include:-

1. Charity begins at home.

2. Our human arrogance and conceit obfuscate our potential for better judgement by not copying the creditable example of so-called animals who all wean their children by not breast-feeding them indefinitely!
3. Add up and re-appraise the foreign aid cash, plus goods, services and soft loans we had contributed to about 196 nations for the past six decades, then visit each one to see what they have done and achieved with this largesse.
4. The purchasing power of most of these countries continue to depreciate on a downward spiral due to mismanagement, illicit misappropriations with capital flight outflows. maladministration, rampant lawlessness within the top tiers of political elites, open corruption with the persecutions of whistle blowers, the overinvoicing of used capital goods for public sectors instead of pricings based on what the rest of the clean world pays, disdain of audit functions for optimisations potential, no credible substitute for maintenance, and maintenance management in

indigenous languages, with complacencies about evolving such.
5. Poor and low standards of public hygiene etc. and contributions to the prevention of ill-health.
6. Poor and low standards of good 24/7 electricity generation with distribution and supplies, food, potable water, jobs opportunities, and housing.
7. Standards of compliances with current laws, rules, and regulations with intermittent essential and desirable optimising reappraisals by proactive surprise auditing.
8. Poor and/or low controls of personal criminal greed by local recipient political elites.
9. Poor and low equal opportunities practices by political leaders – in one West African country of about fourteen internal nations, the President publicly pronounced that he being a Mende man will only accommodate Mendes firstly if not only because they are the only one he knows about.
10. Misogynous tendencies were exposed by another West African political leader who was publicly told by German journalists that his wife had

intimated that he was not the one taking all decisions – people surrounding him also were; he responded by publicly saying "Don't mind her. She is a woman fit for nothing but kitchen and bed".

11. Foreign Aid is unethically misused to secretly bribe recipient countries' political leaders through their agents to conform to donors' geopolitical etc. preferences irrespective of whether or not such recipient countries peoples benefit! In one country, Sierra Leone, after a military coup followed by a palace coup about two decades ago, a former Inspector-General of Police – Bambay Kamara – with about 19 other Sierra Leoneans were arrested, taken to Benguema a town about 21 miles east of Freetown the capital, and massacred without juridical trials!

Numbers 9 and 10 above rob these nations of inputs from all available talents, and adversely affect GDP (gross domestic product).

Inclusive elements of foreign aid support are the deft "nod-nod-wink-wink" malpractices of "we will give you more and may even increase it if you comply with our geo-political priorities, preferences, mutual understandings, subterfuges, and diktats. Donors' commercial banks need such evil financing for their profitable sustenance. Evil capital flight!

The political elites of recipient nations etc. benefit by illicit and untaxed misappropriations into foreign bank accounts whilst their poor continue losing; these donors do not care about the adverse effects of such immoral mismanagement and maladministration anomalies, successfully pretending non-happenstances and particularly ignoring anomalous accountabilities of purchasing and supplies, allied with non-conformances with internal mandatory guidelines such as inherited "STANDING ORDERS".

Other evil tricks include purchasing used/pre-loved/second-hand capital goods and equipments but presenting invoices for "as new" inflated as well in collusion with compatible corrupt sellers! My many experiences of such in early 1974 included one in Freetown, Sierra Leone where after the relevant engineers had presented technical requirements specifications for intended renewals of base load 11 Kilovolts Alternating Current Generators at King Tom Power Station for consequent stepping down via transformers, the politicians in The Energy Ministry thanked the engineers then proceeded to Europe and bought second-hand ones generating at 440 Volts – in blind ignorance – the finishing spray paint were like for new cars with the tell-tale give away of the aluminium alloy cylinder head covers having been sprayed as well – we, engineers do not spray aluminium because it does not rust. Another giveaway was my lubricating oil swab from inside the crankcase was very viscous and jet black in colour instead of nearly new tawny brown colour for a new diesel generator. My unwisely pointing these out did not make me very popular with these "purchasing" politicos. Of course, the generators could not be used at King Tom and any other base-load power station, so had to be installed at electrical stepdown transformer outposts.

Visit King Tom, Falcon Bridge, and King Harman Road Power Stations today November 2021, you will find there are no electricity Generators there because successive Sierra Leone governments since the early seventies till today have poor and low appreciation of maintenance and maintenance management.

Recently during 2021, the Sierra Leone National Audit Offices staffed by civil servants discovered that on their foreign travels, some members of Sierra Leone's President Maada Bio's entourage had submitted and been paid false inflated invoices etc. for services received abroad.

The National Auditor-General and her Deputy detailed and included these in their Annual Report – a statutory duty.

Consequently, President Maada-Bio removed her and her deputy from their posts and placed both under investigations by his appointed 3-Person Tribunal! We await what this Tribunal will be allowed to report – one member of this Tribunal had since resigned and been replaced.

Her Majesty's UK Government continues financial aid to such countries!

CONCLUSION

If Seton During could write such, you my buyer or reader can either do the same or better. The opportunities for beneficial nonfiction books or novellas are already fertilised for you, so, self-motivate and please start writing now.

Seton During
London, UK

www.directcostscutters.com
seton@directcostscutters.com
January 2022.

www.ingramcontent.com/pod-product-compliance
Ingram Content Group UK Ltd.
Pitfield, Milton Keynes, MK11 3LW, UK
UKHW042000230426
12048UKWH00009B/451